A Murder
Has Been
Renounced

by Lee Mueller

©2016

The play will be presented as it appears in published form and the author's intent will be respected in production. No changes, interpolations, or deletions in the text - except where noted in the script or previously discussed with author. No changes to the title of the play can be made for the purpose of production.

**Please note: whenever you wish to make changes to a script, other than those noted, you must always request permission in writing or by email to lee@play-dead.com

Production Requirements:Whenever a play is produced, due authorship credit must be given on all programs, printing and advertising for the play.

Characters

MRS LUDOS – a very proper, no nonsense lady of the estate of Chipping Cleghorn.

MISS HEINSPIELE – a fun loving gentle woman. Perhaps has a slight German accent.

CAPTAIN TRUCAGE – a boisterous gentleman. Slight shady with used car salesmen personality .

MISS MENDACIO – not the brightest bulb but loves social events none the less.

DEIDRE – the maid of the estate. Slightly sarcastic.

NICK DASHELL – private eye. Very hip and modern. Prone to make references no one understands. He not appear smart but underneath his confused look is a very intelligent person.

DARLA DASHELL – Nick's wife. Works as a nurse and works to control Nick's wacky sense of humor.

Setting: Present Day – The Sitting Room of a large estate. Several large stuffed Chairs and a couch. An doorway Upstage right leads out to hallway. A character exiting the doorway goes to the right to the front door and to the left leads off to the stairway.
A doorway upstage left leads off to the kitchen.

Set ideas – the upstage wall can contain a fireplace mantel and bookcase on either side. Perhaps a few paintings adorn the other walls.

Notes on punctuation

A slash (/) indicates a point of interruption in dialogue by actor with the next line. The following line should begin immediately as an overlap of the previous actor's line.

Ellipses …. represent a loss of thought or words at the end of a line

Special thanks to Mo Holkar of Freeformgames.com for technical advice!

Lights up

MRS LUDOS, MISS HEINSPIELE, CAPTAIN TRUCAGE and MISS MENDACIO enter laughing as if in mid conversation. Ludos and Trucage are holding papers. Miss Heinspiele is holding a few 8x5 cards. Mendacio is holding a folded newspaper. The first few lines are spoken normally, that is in the plain voice of the actor as they continue they develop fake British or proper British accents.

LUDOS: And so, everyone knows what to do, correct?

HEINSPIELE: Yes, but.. (*looks around*) Are we all here?

TRUCAGE: Well, I'm here!

HEINSPIELE: Yes, I know *you're* here! I mean, *all* who were invited. We seem a bit short!

TRUCAGE: Well.. we all seem shorter in person. (*laughs at his own joke*)

LUDOS: (*starts accent*) Captain Trucage! Please! Miss Heinspiele is of course referring to our attendance not our altitude!

HEINSPIELE: According to this, (*looks at paper*) there should be more!

MENDACIO: (*starts accent*) Perhaps more will be here. The weather is a bit much this evening.

DEIDRE enters with tray containing a few drinking glasses.

DEIDRE: There's trouble at mill.

LUDOS: There's trouble at what? (*takes glass from tray*)

TRUCAGE: What mill? (*takes glass from tray*)

DEIDRE: It's just an expression. What I mean to say is that I'm afraid the weather has interfered. Not to mention the roads and phone lines.

HEINSPIELE: The roads and phone lines? (*takes glass from tray*)

MENDACIO: She said not to mention them.

DEIDRE: Again, it's just an expression. Mary Westmacott called to say Hillcrest road has washed out and they had to turn around. She began to express her apologies and the line went dead.

LUDOS: How unfortunate. Anyway, we'd better get on with it.

TRUCAGE: Indeed we should.

MEDACIO: Oh yes. It should be fun! (*takes glass from tray lays newspaper down on table*)

LUDOS: If the rest make it here, they will assimilate.

HEINSPIELE: Shall we?

> *LUDOS, HEINSPIELE, TRUCAGE, MEDACIO lift glasses as toast*

TRUCAGE: Once more unto the breech dear friends! Once more!

They drink - each set glasses down various places, table, book shelf etc and cross up right to hallway -

LUDOS: La chasse est ouverte!

> *SOUND CUE Thunder*

> *DEIDRE turns and exits off left doorway   We Hear Knocking on a door (right)*

> *SOUND CUE   Thunder again and LIGHTS flicker*

> *We Hear knocking again – a bit more forceful - A pause -then we hear*

DARLA: *(calling out off stage)* Hello? Any one home?

NICK: *(off)* Hello?!

DARLA: *(off)* Hello?

NICK: *(off)* Hola? *(beat)* Bon-jour? *(beat)* Guten-tag?!

DARLA: *(off)* Seriously?

NICK and DARLA DASHALL peek into room from right side of hallway archway.

NICK: Anyone? Bueler? Bueler?

DARLA: Stop it Nick.

NICK: (*pointing off to left*) Maybe they're upstairs.

They enter wet from rain. Both are wearing coats. NICK stamps feet shakes umbrella. He is wearing a Deerstalker style hat – the look around the room.

DARLA: There's no one in here. (*looking at empty glasses*) But there was! Looks like there was a celebration recently.

NICK: (*picks up empty glass*) And it's still warm!

DARLA: (*sighs at Nick*) At least it's warm in here.

NICK: So, what are the rules for wandering into someone's home unannounced? Do you go looking and find them or.. just kinda hang until they find you.

DARLA: Let's just remain here and find out.

NICK: All those in favor say aye or I. Because *I* certainly am not going back outside! It's wretched out there. And wet too! (*removes hat shaking it to dry it off*)

DARLA: At least the lights are on so..and who just leaves the door open?

NICK: Well, people in this neck of the upper echelon do all sorts of wacky things. They can afford to!

DARLA: *(checking her cellphone)* But they can't afford a decent cell tower! Still no signal!

NICK: Maybe they can afford us a little accommodation. Like a phone. Like real one with wires and stuff that plug into the wall.

DARLA: Seriously Nick! Look at us! Would you let people dressed like us, use the phone?

DEIDRE enters from doorway left holding a candle in a candle stick and tray under his arm.

DEIDRE: Oh hello! You've made it!

DARLA: No! We're not..

NICK: *(interrupting)* Yes! Yes we did! Make it that is! Weather's not fit for man nor fowl!

DEIDRE: I'm sorry sir? *(setting candle stick down)*

NICK: Why? It's not your fault it's raining.

DEIDRE: No sir. I meant, *sorry* as in.. I did not hear what sir was saying.

DEIDRE continues on gathering up empty glasses on her tray

DARLA: Uhh..Sir was saying the weather is quite foul.

NICK: No, Darla. I said the weather's not fit for man nor fowl. Fowl as in..you know. I was going for a pun.

DEIDRE: Yes, most hilarious I'm sure. Pardon me, but I take it this is part of the....milieu[1]?

NICK: The mill what?

DEIDRE: No. Part of the whole... .you know. *(sighs)* Very good. I'll play along. *(clears throat)* May I be of some service?

NICK: Service? Yea, that would be awesome! Because our phones definitely have no service out in this neck of the woods.

DEIDRE: Yes, we are rather remote here at the Chipping Cleghorn estate. Communications are an issue.

NICK: So are you the... maid? No offense, I'm just assuming, I mean you're dressed like what I'm imagine a maid would be dressed like. With the whole maid like look... and the tray with the whole tidying up thing.

DEIDRE: Uh.. yes. Sure. The maid. My name is Deidre.

---

1 (mill-you)

NICK: Deidre? Of course it is. I mean it's very maid-esqe. It always Deidre, Helga or Mitzi or something exotic.

DARLA: Actually Deidre, the fact is, we're not actually... what I mean is, we sort of.. just walked in. We tried the doorbell and it didn't seem to be working and then we tried knocking and well, forgive us... I apologize! We're Nick and Darla Dashall. We ran into some trouble a ways back down the road.

NICK: Maybe like a clogged fuel line, or fuel pump, fuel filter... you know something fuel related... where fuel is not getting to the.. fuel thing. Any-who,saw the lights on here and well, here we are..

DARLA: Two soaking wet strangers dripping all over your floor.

DEIDRE: I see. The stranded travelers. Very good. Nice variation. May I take your coats? (*sets tray with glasses down*)

DARLA: (*confused*) Variation?

NICK: Absolutely! Thanks!

> NICK removes coat and is wearing a "Sherlock Holmes" style costume with Houndstooth Coat With attached cape hand it over to DEIDRE. DARLA removes her coat and has a nurses uniform with several splatters

of fake blood on it and her white nylons have several rips.

DEIDRE: (*to Nick*) Very fitting costume might I say.

NICK: Of course you can say! (*Nick puts back on the Deerstalker cap*) But can you guess?

DEIDRE: I believe I can. It's elementary! No offense, I'm just assuming, I mean you're dressed like what I'm imagine...

NICK: Spot on Deeds! That's correct! (*beat*) Victorian Vampire! I had some fangs... (*searches pockets*) .. I think I dropped them somewhere along the way. But anyway, my dear wife Darla here is the classic B-movie Zombie Nurse! Or I should say *was.* (*looking at Darla's face*) Looks like the rain sort of created a buzz kill.

DARLA: Anyway Deidre, do you think we could use your phone, we won't be any bother.

DEIDRE: Phone? I'm sorry but the phone service is a tad spotty. The lines may bee down due to the weather. From what I'm lead to believe some of the roads are impassible as well.

NICK: Impassible roads and impossible phones? Are you sure?

DEIDRE: Quite sure sir. What I am not sure about are the lights. The power in the area has been fluctuating and lights have been flickering. I've gathered candles in case.

NICK: Wow bummer. Hey, do you think I might wash my hands somewhere? They're a bit greasy and oily and fuely... in case we have to use the candles. I don't want to.. combust or anything.

DARLA: And maybe try the phone again. Just in case.

DEIDRE: Sure, we can try. If you would like to follow me.

DEIDRE begins to cross Stage Left Door to exit

NICK: Thanks Dee! Be right with you! (*starts to cross stops and turns to Darla*) Darla, yea I know this is a bit of a drag, you know with the car and rain and all..

DARLA: Just a "bit" of a drag Nick? No, this is off the scale! You talk me into going to some nerd fest Costume party. But we're stuck in the middle of nowhere! I could be home, warm and dry. Watching TV or reading a book. But I'm not. I'm cold and wet standing in a strange place dressed in a strange costume!

NICK: Darla please. More sunshine! Less flippancy! (*exits*)

DARLA: (*yelling after him*) Zombies are supposed to be flippant Nick! (*quieter to herself*) There is no sunshine for the walking dead health care workers! Flippancy ensues. I mean who wouldn't be a tad flippant in this situation?

(*beat*) Are you talking to yourself Darla? Why yes. Yes I am! (*wanders around room looking*) It's raining buckets outside and we stumble into a big old creepy house. The lines are down. Roads are washed out. A maid named Deidre. We've walked into a bad cliché! The one that begins with the line, It was a dark and stormy night. (beat) Tonight! On a very special episode of S*uspense Mystery theatre.* (*notices newspaper on table. Picks it up, sits down on couch*) Cue Miss Marple!

       DARLA opens paper to read. Headline on front in big letters "Crazed Killer On The Loose"

MRS LUDOS and MISS MENDACIO enter from hallway up right -DARLA remains still hiding behind paper – Ludos and Mendacino speaking with British accents (not necessarily good accents)

LUDOS: (*as she is entering*) And I said, Miss Haversham, you know I always take my tea black with two sugars. I don't know why you believe I have always taken it white.

MENDACIO Speaking of tea, I just read somewhere, that they have found her body.

LUDOS: Where?

MENDACIO It was in the newspaper.

       DARLA peaks from behind newspaper around to read headline, Looks shocked.

LUDOS: No, dear, I mean "where" did they find her body?

MENDACIO I'm not sure. Some here. Some there. In several places.

LUDOS: That's her all over. Poor Miss Haversham. You know, I have also heard that Captain Trucage was the last person to see her alive. In one piece that is.

MENDACIO Hopefully he won't be the last to see us alive! I do find him rather.. mysterious.

LUDOS: Oh yes as do I. Under his seemingly harmless appearance and manner, there could be a evil perpetrator lurking. I would not want to be left alone with him!

MENDACIO Yes! I do hope the others will make it here this evening!

> DARLA stands up

MENDACIO: *(noticing Darla)* Oh splendid! Nurse Christie! You've made it!

DARLA: Who? Yes, but no, I'm not... (*begins to cross toward Ludos*)

MENDACIO Mrs Ludos! It just occurred to me!

DARLA: ..actually.. my husband and I..

LUDOS: Heavens yes! We left poor Miss Heinspiele alone upstairs with Captain Trucage! What were we thinking!

MENDACIO: Tea! We were thinking about tea!

DARLA: Hello? Excuse (/) me but...

LUDOS: We must go at once!

   MRS LUDOS and MISS MENDACIO run off to hallway up right

DARLA:(*continuing only to herself*) ..I'm not .. whoever... whatever! (*short pause*) Are you talking to yourself again Darla?

   NICK enters from doorway left wiping off his hands with towel

NICK: Who are you talking to Darla?

DARLA: Yes, exactly!

NICK: I'm sorry, did I miss something?

DARLA: Yes! You missed quite a lot! Like the two weird tea ladies and the mutilated body.

NICK: What? (*looks around*) I was only gone for a few minutes!! What happened?

DARLA: Some ladies came in here talking about tea and something about some woman... Miss Haversham. They found her all over. And then they saw me and called me Nurse Chrissy or somebody! And suddenly they realized they left someone alone upstairs with the guy.   Look at this! (*hands him newspaper*)

NICK: What is this?

DARLA: It's called a *newspaper*. It's what people used to get news and information from before the inter-webs!

NICK: (*looks at paper -reading out loud*) "Crazed killer on the loose. In or about the area of Chipping Cleghorn...

DARLA: Yea, I've heard that name somewhere.

NICK: I've heard the name Foghorn Leghorn! But he's a big rooster. Wait a tick! Cleghorn? Didn't Deidre mention that? As in it was name of this area?

DARLA: Yes I think she did, but I know that name from something else.

NICK: Anyway. (*reading*) "A string of homicides are believed to be the act of one individual whose identity and whereabouts remains unknown. So be on the lookout!" (*beat*) *On the lookout* for what? Who writes this stuff?

DARLA: The tea ladies were saying something about..who was it? Mr...Trucage? He was the last person to see this Haversham person. And that this Heins..spill was alone upstairs with him. And they panicked and ran off.

NICK: Who ran off?

DARLA: And it's odd that one of the ladies acted like she knew me!

NICK: Who knew you?

DARLA: One of the Tea ladies! Aren't you listening?

NICK: I'm trying! Somebody was the last person to see somebody (/) and then...

DARLA: No! Listen! This Trucage .. was the last person to see this Haversham lady. Suddenly they realized he was alone with this Heins lady and they ran off!

NICK: OK. Let's try this again. (*beat*) *Who* ran off?

DARLA: The tea ladies!

NICK: (*beat*) So, where does the "tea" come into play?

DARLA: No where! Forget the tea! They were saying Haversham was found in pieces after seeing this Trucage and they left someone alone with (/) him and..

NICK: I know! "They ran off!" I remember that part. Where did they run off to?

DARLA: *(points)* Upstairs I guess! I don't know. Maybe we should get out of this crazy place and just wait in the car.

NICK: Or maybe we should do something!

DARLA: Do something? Do what?

NICK: What else can we do? We can't go anywhere! It's torrential down pour! The cell signal doesn't work! The regular phone doesn't work! The car doesn't work! But me? I work! I should do what I do best!

DARLA: That's what I was afraid of! You want to play a detective!

NICK: No, I'm a Victorian Vampire!

DARLA: No Nick dear! Not tonight! I'm talking *real* life!

The lights flicker off and then back on. A scream is heard off stage in distance

NICK: Right! And that sounded like a *real* scream! Time for me to run off!

NICK runs off to hallway up right –

DARLA: *(as he is running)* But Nick! Maybe we should wait to (/) find out if....

NICK: No time for this! I need to find out about that!
(*NICK exits*)

DARLA: *(sighs)* OK Yea. Find out Nick. Find out if
maybe *this* is the house on haunted hill. (*crosses back
looking around*) Maybe some eccentric rich lunatic invited
everyone here tonight and will pay out a fortune to
whoever spends the night. And lives. And then 13 ghosts
will appear. (*crosses over toward left doorway*) Or maybe
this is the one where we're on Elm street or this is the
home of Mother Bates and the crazed Killer is actually..

     *DEIDRE enters quickly through Left Doorway
holding large knife – there is blood on her hand*

DARLA: Ah! (*very startled*) OH! Deidre! You scared the
life out of me!

DEIDRE: Every so sorry ma'am. Not my intention. I
thought I heard someone speaking and I thought the
others were in here.

DARLA: Others? (*looks around*) No. No others. Earlier,
yes, there were others, but now... just me. Again. By
myself. Talking that is. To my...(*noticing blood on
DEIDRE hand*) ..self. (*nervous*) Is that uh... blood by
chance?

DEIDRE: Yes, a very good chance indeed. I was
preparing some slices and when the lights went I
apparently slipped and nicked the dickens out of my
finger.

DARLA: *(relaxes)* Oh my. Let me take a look at it!

> *DARLA reaches out for his hand, DEIDRE pulls back a little hesitant.*

DARLA: Don't worry. I really do have a medical background. Seriously. *(she takes his hand to look at it)* This was my husbands idea for a costume. *(examines his hand)* Yea, that's a nasty cut there. We should run some cold water on it. Clean it up. Do you have gauze or a band aids?

DEIDRE: Yes, of course. Out in the kitchen. Right this way. *(starts to exit out left doorway)*

DARLA: *(follows then stops)* Oh wait! My husband! We heard a scream and he went..

DEIDRE: Did you say scream?

DARLA: Yes. And my husband went to investigate. You see, in real life (/) my husband is a...

> *MISS HEINSPIELE suddenly enters from Left Doorway*

HEINSPIELE: OH! Deidre! There you are! We were just upstairs wondering when the treats and light refreshments would be ready?

DEIDRE: I was working on it.

18

HEINSPIELE: We were also wondering if anyone else made it. (*looking at Darla*) Oh good! You're here! Love the costume!

DARLA: Yes, I'm .. uh..here. Did you say *Heinspiele*?

HEINSPIELE: Yes! Ever so glad to meet you dear. (*back to DEIDRE*) What should I tell them? An hour or so?

DEIDRE: Yes. That would be sufficient. I should have everything ready.

HEINSPIELE: Wonderful! I'll go back upstairs and let them know! (*to Darla*) So glad you could make it. Frightful weather!

     HEINSPIELE cross and exits up hallway exits to left.

DARLA: (*as Heinspiele crosses*) Yes.. it's very frightful. (*to DEIDRE*) I guess she's not in that much danger

DEIDRE: Only some of the time. (*beat*) Shall we tend to the matter at hand? (*raising up bloody hand*)

DARLA: (*sighs*) Sure! Why not!

     DEIDRE and DARLA exit out Left door.

     SOUND: Thunder. LIGHTS flicker

TRUCAGE silently enters through RIGHT doorway. He looks around to make sure no one sees or hears him. He crosses over to Left Door and listens for a moment. He crosses back center and reaches in jacket pocket and removes necklace – looking closely at and smiles. As he speaks he does so very broadly and dramatically as if performing

TRUCAGE: Keep me out the loop will you! Ha! I'll show you how to win this venture! Nothing but a stage? Maybe. But in this stage of the event, I know my exits and entrances and can play many parts. And win many a tourney!

SOUND: Knock at front door (off)

TRUCAGE looks around nervously. Starts to put jewelry back in pocket but stops. Quickly crosses over to couch, lifts cushion and hides necklaces under it.

At this moment DARLA peers out from doorway LEFT

DARLA: *(speaking back as if to DEIDRE)* No, It sounded as if it were coming from out here and.. *(seeing Trucage)* Oh! Hello!

TRUCAGE: Hellooooo nurse!

DARLA: I thought I heard someone.

TRUCAGE: Someone? Yes! That someone would be me. *(crossing to Darla)* And to who do I have the pleasure?

DARLA: Well, the pleasure would be telling you I'm.. *Mrs.* Dashell. Mrs. Darla Dashall.

TRUCAGE: Is that so? A Mrs.? Such a shame!

DARLA: Probably. And you are?

TRUCAGE: Captain Montgomery Trucage! You may call me Monty.

DARLA: Ah! Yes, I've heard *about* you.

TRUCAGE: You have? Splendid! Splendid! But you have me at a disadvantage dear Darla, I know nothing of you! Tsk tsk that I should stand here and wonder? Prey let us solve one mystery shall we?

DARLA: One mystery would be.. why are you talking that way?

TRUCAGE: And how do you wish me to speak?

DARLA: Maybe a little more present day, a little less Jane Austen.

TRUCAGE: Very good Darla! And what is your role this evening?

DARLA: My role? Well, I thought it would be obvious by my appearance. *(beat)* Tax accountant.

   SOUND: Knock at front door (off)

TRUCAGE: Ah! Yes. Speaking of taxing, I should get the door! Won't be a moment.

Turns crosses to up right hallway –
TRUCAGE: Yes! Yes! Coming! (*exits to right off stage*)

DARLA turns and crosses to Left Doorway as if to exit – but hesitates to listen as:

TRUCAGE: (*off*) Hello! Welcome! (*beat*) Oh! It's you!

Two quick gunshots (off) interrupt. Darla reacts in horror not sure what to do

DEIDRE enters from doorway left. Her hand is wrapped in dish towel.

DEIDRE: Is someone knocking at the door?

DARLA points toward upstage Right doorway -crossing to DEIDRE

DARLA: No! No knocking. (*waves hands gesturing to be quiet – then whispering loudly pointing*) Shots! Gun shots!   Out there! Shhhh!

DEIDRE: Shots? (*begins to cross up right*)

DARLA: (*stops DEIDRE -still whispering*) At the door! There's someone with a gun! I think they shot Trucage!

DEIDRE: But *gun* shots? Interesting.

DARLA: I need to find my husband!

DEIDRE: Where is he?

DARLA: He went to see about the scream!

DEIDRE: Ah yes! The scream.

DARLA: Now he needs to see about the shots.

DEIDRE: Yes. The shots. (*calmly crosses to exit out Door left*)

DARLA: Wait! (*whispering loudly*) Where are you going? Someone may have been shot!

DEIDRE: You're a nurse. *You* see to the victim, I must see to the vegetables. (*exits*)

> DARLA turns slowly and takes a few steps toward up right doorway.

DARLA: Seriously? *(beat)* Right! I should probably go and check... (*takes a few steps and stops*) But.. wait! What if they're still out there... with a gun. (*beat -goes and picks up candle stick – removes candle and tosses it*) OK! (*loudly*) I have a candle stick and I'm not afraid to use it! (*takes a few more steps – to herself*) If there *is* someone there, they're being awfully quiet. Maybe they left? Ran away? How do you know? I don't. You really should go and see. OK I will.

Darla takes quiet steps, sneaking toward up right doorway. Just as she reaches doorway and begins to peak around raising candle stick– NICK enters suddenly -they startle each other

DARLA: NICK!!

NICK: DARLA!!

DARLA grabs him and pulls him away from doorway

DARLA: *(whispering loudly)* There's someone with a gun!

NICK: *(whispering loudly)* Gun? Where?

DARLA: *(whispering loudly)* Out there!! At the door!!

Nick steps back and looks out doorway toward right.

NICK: *(speaks normal volume)* Out there? There's no one at the door.

DARLA: What about the body!?

NICK: The body? *(looks around left and right)* What body?

DARLA: What? *(Crosses and looks out doorway)* The body of the guy that was shot! They shot him!

NICK: Shot who?

DARLA: Trucage! (*crosses back into room*)

NICK: Why does all this stuff happen when I leave?!
(*crosses to Darla*)

 DARLA: He was just in here! I saw him *here* in this
room. We spoke and someone knocked...at the door. He
went out there to answer it. He said something to.. and
then gunshots.!!

NICK. Hang on. Rewind! You're sure it was Trucage you
saw?

DARLA: Yes! He told me his name. We talked for a
minute. He was totally smarmy.

NICK: So I've heard.

DARLA: Didn't you *hear* the shots?

NICK: I heard something. Maybe it was the shots, maybe
the knocking.

DARLA: What about the scream?

NICK: One of your "tea" ladies lost something. A
necklace or something. She screamed. You know how
you girls are with your accessories. What's with the
candle stick?

DARLA: It's an accessory. Protection. From people with guns . Who knock at the door. And shoot people.

NICK: So where are these people? The people with guns?

DARLA: I don't know. You're the detective. You tell me!
NICK: Good answer. Or... question. Whatever the case may be.

DARLA: So what is the case?

NICK: Well, the case of the disappearing necklace... and...

DARLA: ..disappearing shooter and shootie.

NICK: Shall we start looking?

DARLA: After you.

NICK: Me? Ladies first. Ladies with candlesticks that is.

DARLA gives him a look

NICK: All right! Very well.

NICK exits right follow by Darla
Lights down.

LIGHTS UP - MRS LUDOS, MISS HEINSPIELE and MISS MENDACIO are seated sipping from tea cups. They continue speaking with faux British accents except where noted.

LUDOS: But I don't understand! Where could he have gotten to?

HEINSPIELE: Well, he was there one moment and the next.. not! Very strange!

MENDACIO: Most strange indeed. I should say! *(beat)* I should also ask, who are we talking about? Captain Trucage or that strange detective like person?

HEINSPIELE: Well, I suppose both at this point.

LUDOS: Yes, and more to the point, where did this strange detective person come from?

MENDACIO: He came because of your scream I believe.

LUDOS: *(drops accent for this line)* No, I mean for the evening's festivities. I don't recall a detective. *(beat)* Yet.

HEINSPIELE: But I'm thankful he is here..or was. That nasty business with the necklace

MENDACIO: Where could it have gotten to?

LUDOS: More like.. who could have gotten to it!

HEINSPIELE: Maybe this detective fellow will find your necklace. Awfully convenient if you ask me ! Necklace disappears and a strange detective appears!

DEIDRE enters

HEINSPIELE: Oh Deidre, we were just wondering, have you seen our gentlemen?

DEIDRE: Your gentlemen?

LUDOS: She means the fellow parading as a detective.

DEIDRE: Oh him. Actually he prefers to a "Victorian" vampire.

MENDACIO: Vampire?

DEIDRE: I believe he went to investigate the scream.

HEINSPIELE: The scream?

DEIDRE: And his wife, the zombie, went to investigate the gun shots.

LUDOS: (*no accent*) Gun shots?

MENDACIO: Zombie ?

DEIDRE: I believe she is a nurse in real life. Said she was. Bandaged up my hand.

HEINSPIELE: Ah that would be Nurse Christy!

LUDOS: (*no accent*) What gun shots?

DEIDRE: The gun shots from the doorway.

HEINSPIELE: You remember Nurse Christie don't you dear? We met earlier.

LUDOS: (*resumes accent*) What of these gunshots? Who was shot?

DEIDRE: I believe Darla was under the assumption that Captain Trucage may have been involved somehow. Perhaps being the recipient of said shots. She went to see.

MENDACIO: I don't recall zombies being a part of the evening. How entertaining! This really adds to the evening doesn't it?

LUDOS: How Miss Mendacio?! How does this add to the evening?

MENDACIO: Well, first your necklace turns ups missing and then the detective appears from nowhere. And now gunshots!

HEINSPIELE: I guess she has a point. It notches it up from the standard fair we're accustom to.

LUDOS: That it does, but it's just that... it's progressing rather quickly! We have had treats and light refreshments yet.

HEINSPIELE: Who cares? I for one grow tired of the same old thing. Our annual gatherings have become.. predictable! I vote we continue on! Who knows what other frivolities may occur? I mean, here we were worried about the evening, the weather and everyone canceling!

MENDACIO: Now we have gunshots, vampires and zombies. Oh my!

HEINSPIELE: Perhaps it's like they say, less is more! Speaking of more, you know dearies, it's just about the Red Hour!

DEIDRE: Shall I get the light refreshments before anything else happens? *(begins to cross to exit)*

HEINSPIELE: Thank you Deidre, you've been an absolute dear this evening. Allow me to see to it! *(crosses to exit off left)* I brought some ladyfingers this evening, I'll just pop in and see to them!

 (Heinspiele exits and Deidre remains THE LIGHTS BLINK)

LUDOS: Great! That's all we need now is for the lights to go out.

30

MENDACIO: It would be fitting though don't you think Miss Ludos?

LUDOS: It could be! Especially during that dreadful musical convocation.

MENDACIO: You mean The Red Hour?

LUDOS: Do stop referring to it as such. You know I abhor obscure references!

DEIDRE: Shall I do the honors ma'am?

LUDOS: Sure. Why not. Let's get this bloody thing going.

MENDACIO: Shouldn't we wait for Mrs Heinspiele? She does so enjoy it!

LUDOS: And since I do not enjoy it, I will go and tell her. You may continue.

LUDOS crosses and exits left

DEIDRE walks over and turns on music player – CD or Ipod – old cheezey instrumental music comes on (such as "Adios" by Xavier Cugat or the Bollywood song " Jaan Pehchan Ho" by Mohammed Rafi or "A Walk in the Black Forest" - Horst Jankowski -) as music begins -DEIDRE remains upstage watching. MRS MENDACIO spins with an interpretive style dance.

MISS LUDOS re enters and paces around not really wanting to participate. This goes on for a while – NICK and DARLA enter from RIGHT and stand for a moment somewhat amused at the scene. NICK relents and begins his own little interpretive dance, DARLA tries to stop him. MRS LUDOS finally sees Nick and Darla and waves furiously to DEIDRE to turn off the music. MUSIC STOPS.

NICK: Well, don't stop on our account! Party people in the house! La dee da dee, we like to party, We don't cause trouble, we don't bother nobody!

DARLA: Nick! Please! Stop!

MENDACIO: We weren't supposed to stop! Not yet! It's the red hour!

NICK: Red hour? Like from episode 21 of Star Trek?

DEIDRE: Unfortunately. It's all part of the evening. The festivities! You know.

NICK: Oh I get ya. The festivities. A little chance to bust a move. Watch each other whip and nae nae. I'm hip.

LUDOS: Mr Detective! We were wondering where in the world you got to!

NICK: Me? Well, I *got to* look all over the place! High and low for the signs of any shooting or any body.. that is as in any *body*, not just anybody... but an actual, you know, body.

MENDACIO: Did you find the necklace?

NICK: Necklace? Uh... no, not as such. Because I was thinking, in lieu of the necklace, I'd look into the alleged shooting and possible homicide. Maybe it's me but...

LUDOS: No, no. I apologize for Mrs Mendacio by all means, you should look into the *shooting* first and foremost! I would say that is important, wouldn't you Mrs Mendacio?

MENDACIO: Oh yes! Yes indeed! Shooting. Yes.

NICK: That's not to say, I couldn't look for the necklace as well. I'm not having much luck finding anyone with bullet holes.

DARLA: Speaking of which, have you ladies seen Captain Trucage by chance?

MENDACIO: Why yes! Of course I have seen him. On several occasions!

LUDOS: I believe she is referring to an occasion that would exist in the realm of very recently.

DARLA: Such as the last 30 minutes or so..realm.

LUDOS: I believe I can help. Captain Trucage was upstairs with us earlier in the evening. The "us" would be myself, Miss Mendacio and Mrs Heinspiele. We were all admiring the new portrait in the west hallway. Then I believe we retired to our respective rooms to freshen up. Miss Mendacio and myself came down here.. where we met you, *(indicates Darla)* and we have not seen him since.

DARLA: And Mrs Heinspiele? Where is she?

MENDACIO: She went out to the kitchen to get her fingers.

NICK: Oh. Are they missing too?

MENDACIO: Oh I hope not! *(walks upstage with back to audience as if checking something)*

DARLA: Nick really! Can't you be serious for one minute? There's something weird going on in this place.

NICK: I am being serious. And seriously, we must consider the fact that *you* dear were the last person to see Trucage! Alive or otherwise. I consider that weird! Not to mention, your tale of the gunshots!

DARLA: Nick I am telling you it happened just like I said. I came out of the kitchen, because I heard someone talking, it was Trucage.. Someone knocked on the front door! *(she crosses right toward doorway)* He walked out there, opened the door... I heard him say something like

"Oh it's you." Which is exactly what every victim says when they answer a door!

NICK: And then?

DARLA: And then gunshots!

NICK: And then?

DARLA: And then Deidre came out of the kitchen.

DEIDRE: That's right. Speaking of kitchen, I should get back out there and see if she's found her fingers. (*crosses and exits*)

LUDOS: Oh yea please do! Who knows who else or what else will turn up missing!

  DEIDRE crosses and exits – MENDACIO turns back and crosses down to group

NICK: So, to make sure I am not missing anything, you heard a voice. You came from the kitchen out here into the ..the ..whatever this room is... what is this room by the way.. Living room? Drawing Room? Parlor?

LUDOS: We refer to it as the sitting room.

NICK: Sitting? I stand corrected. Anyway, you say you saw Captain Trucage in here. You spoke with him. "Hello, how are you?" "I am fine." "Blah blah blah". Suddenly, there's was a knock at the door.

We Hear a KNOCK on the door (off stage)

NICK: *(cont.)* Probably like that! *(walks over to doorway)* Trucage walks over and goes out to answer it.

NICK exits as if to answer door.

DARLA: *(alarmed)* Nick wait! *(quickly cross to stop him)*

THE LIGHTS Go out.

LUDOS: I had a feeling that would happen! It's probably the breakers out in the kitchen . Bad weather always trips them. A little water here, Some little wires there. Darkness ensues.

MENDACIO: Shall I go see about the breakers? You know in the kitchen? I can take care of it.

LUDOS: If you can manage! There's a utility box on the south wall. Miss Heinspiele can help you.

MENDACIO: No problem. I'll take care go take care of it.

MENDACIO feels her way out exiting

DARLA: Nick? (beat) Nick! Are you all right?

NICK: *(off stage)* I think so. Having a bit of an issue seeing at the moment.

DARLA: Who's at the door?

NICK: *(off)* Who's on the floor?

DARLA: No Nick! I said the door!

NICK: Yes. Yes, I am at the door. I'm trying to find the handle. *(beat)* I think I have it! Yes! *(beat)* No wait! This is not a door. It's the hall tree. I found our coats if we need them.

DARLA: Oh for the love of Pete!

NICK: If whoever is knocking, if you could knock again?

    (A few more knocks)

NICK: Brilliant. That helps. *(beat)* Ah! I think found something handle-ish. Might be it. Maybe not.

DARLA: Don't you have your flashlight?

NICK: Flashlight?

DARLA: Yes. You always carry it.

NICK: I do? *(beat)* Oh! Right! I do! Searching the pockets now. *(beat)* Not that one. Wait! I think.. no. That's a pen. And my car keys. Found some mints. Where did I get mints?

DARLA: Nick! Forget the mints.

NICK: Right! Mints forgotten! Wait! What's this? Ha! Score! Let there be light! I see the door! Opening now! The eagle has landed. *(beat)* Oh! It's you!

DARLA: *(waits a few beats)* Nick? Who's at the door Nick?!

NICK: Do you mean, besides me?

DARLA: Yes!

> *The LIGHTS come back up*

LUDOS: Miss Mendacio must have found the target.

> *DARLA crosses toward doorway. She stops suddenly and slowly begins backing up into the room. MR TRUCAGE enters -he appears disheveled. There is a gag (handkerchief) around his mouth and his hands are bound together in front. LUDOS and slightly -gasp etc... NICK assists TRUCAGE by removing gag -which comes off quite easily.*

TRUCAGE: Thanks ever so much old boy! Bit of a sticky wicket, if I do say!

LUDOS: Captain Trucage! What on earth happened?

TRUCAGE: Not sure! There was a knock at (/) the door..

NICK: We know. We've seen this bit a few times now.

TRUCAGE: (confused)   I'm sorry? Seen what bit?

DARLA: Never mind Captain, we all know about the knock at the door. Please tell us what happened next. Like who was at the door when you answered it.

   MENDACIO enters

TRUCAGE: Oh yes that! Well, let's see.. forgive me, my head is still spinning and... well, uh... the door, yes! (to Ludos) I say, do you remember..what was his name... Mr. Quincannon from the outing last year? Well as sure as I'm standing here, I thought it was him. And before you can say, Bob's your Uncle, I was grabbed in a restraining manner. A bag placed over my head.
   (a few beats)

DARLA: And then?

TRUCAGE: And then?

NICK: Loud noises maybe? Kind of like... bang bang! Maybe gunshots?!

TRUCAGE: Right! Yes! I do recall some noises now that you mention it!I As I said, a bag was placed over my head. I could not see. Perhaps there were.. yes! Of course, the gunshots. I imagine it was a diversionary tactic! I'm not quite sure why it was there. All I know is that I was bound up and left in what I believe to be the garden shed.

LUDOS: Oh deary me! Sounds like you have had quite a kerfuffle! Filled with assorted rough housing! Here, have a seat poor fellow. You'll be right as rain in no time.

LUDOS leads TRUCAGE over to sit down.

TRUCAGE: It was frightening I tell you! It's getting so a fellow can't answer the door anymore!

Ludos, Trucage and Mendacio quietly stage talk upstage left as DARLA leads NICK downstage right to talk out of earshot of the three.

DARLA: OK! That's it! I'm done! Done with these people and this whole fruit loop gathering!

NICK: But Darla, we've (/) only...

DARLA: But Darla nothing! This is not normal. These people are not normal. This creepy place, not normal! This situation. These stories. These accents! Nothing that is going on here is...

NICK: Normal! Right. I think you've made your point and normally, I would say you're right. But there's too many loose ends.

DARLA: No loose ends Nick. No loose ends! Just some story about a bag and a garden shed. He wasn't shot. There's no dead body. He sitting over there just as sure as you please! The end is no longer loose!

NICK and DARLA silently converse as we now hear the other conversation

TRUCAGE: Sorry everyone for the worry!

MENDACIO: It's fine. Everything is.. fine now.

TRUCAGE: Good. Thank you Miss Mendacio. If it weren't for that peculiar business!

LUDOS: It's all peculiar business, if you ask me. Those people are peculiar. This situation. These stories. Everything is peculiar.

TRUCAGE: Spot on I say! And strange having that nurse and the detective. It's a wonder they made it in this weather.

LUDOS: I wonder what they're talking about over there?

NICK and DARLA resume as the other three silently converse.

DARLA: I wonder what they're talking about over there?

NICK: Probably how fortunate they are that we arrived. You know, taking charge of the situation.

DARLA: Situation? What situation?

NICK: Well, the uh.... the....you know. Trucage thing.

DARLA: There was no Trucage thing. He was lost and now he is found.

NICK: And was blind but now... I see there's more going on here than meets the eye!

DARLA: And I don't like what I see! It's like we're in some bad B movie. You know the one with the amateur acting and the plot you've seen a million times. The car breaks down in the rain. The large estate. The Fellini characters. It's been done to death.

NICK: Possibly, but I'm still wondering about the sub plot. If Trucage was grabbed when he answered the door and then bound up in a shed, why? And more to the point *Who*?

DARLA: Who cares? Let's go.

NICK: No, let's think about it Darla! Let's use the little gray cells. Who knocked on the door? Who grabbed him and fired off shots? I can vouch for the ladies whereabouts. We were upstairs and you were down here with Deidre and Trucage. That's everyone. And if that's everyone... then who did it? It seems we have an extra guest.

  NICK and DARLA silently converse as we now hear the other conversation

LUDOS: If that's the case, then it seems we have extra guests.

MENDACIO: Should we arrange for extra refreshments?

LUDOS: Speaking of refreshments, I do wonder whats become of Mrs Heinspiele?

TRUCAGE: I'm sure she's just fine.

NICK and DARLA resume as the other three silently converse.

DARLA: This is not a "who done it"! Nothing has been done to anyone.

DEIDRE enters

DEIDRE: Excuse me, I don't mean to interrupt but... I believe Mrs Heinspiele is dead.

LUDOS: What?

TRUCAGE: Good Lord!

MENDACIO: Really?

DEIDRE: Yes.

NICK: *(to Darla)* What were you saying dear?

LIGHTS DOWN

LIGHTS UP

CAPTAIN TRUCAGE is pacing. MRS LUDOS is seated on couch with MISS MEDACINO as the act opens. DEIDRE stands upstage.

LUDOS: Well, this turned out quite... interesting.

MENDACIO: But Miss Heinspiele?

TRUCAGE: It's the way the worm turns.

MENDACIO: But.. Miss Heinspiele?

LUDOS: I'm lead to believe it was poison in the ladyfingers. Perhaps meant for one of us.

TRUCAGE: Do you assume it was placed there, by one of us?

LUDOS: Or one of *them.*

TRUCAGE: You mean Shifty Sherlock and Nurse Ratchett? What are they doing out there anyway?

DEIDRE: Investigating I believe. Scouring for clues.

LUDOS: Deidre, If I'm not mistaken, you were out in the kitchen with Miss Heinspeile.

DEIDRE: Yes but...

MENDACIO: But Miss Heinspiele.

LUDOS: Why do you keep saying, *But Miss Heinspiele?*

MENDACIO: Because we were worried that Captain Trucage was ..

LUDOS: Was what? Captain Trucage is right here, isn't he? Quite alive?

TRUCAGE: Yes, yes he is. If I do say so myself. Close call at the door earlier. And as I said, I believe it was a diversion, to lure me away.

MENDACIO: Oh, I see! A diversion! A red salmon!

LUDOS: I believe you mean *red herring*.

TRUCAGE: Well, it's all fishy if you ask me. A person looking like Quincannon grabs and bounds me. Fires off a pistol and throws me in the shed! To what end?

MENDACIO: Well, I would think to Miss Heinspiele's end! It wasn't you in trouble Captain. But Miss Heinspiele! But maybe that's just me.

LUDOS: That *is just you* with all your nonsense utterances this evening.

MENADCINO: I will have you know Miss Ludos I do not utter non sense!

LUDOS: It's all utter non sense! I vote we bring this all to an end.

MENDACIO: You can't do that! We've just started!

LUDOS: Started? Nothing has gone to plan! Why go on?

    NICK enters

NICK: Hello, excuse me?

LUDOS: Yes? Go on.

NICK: As you know, we have a bit of a situation here. Actually, a bit of a bummer situation. Bummer in the sense that.. we have what appears to be a homicide and to top it off, we have no way to contact the authorities.

TRUCAGE: Authorities? My dear man, we thought *you* were the authorities!

DEIDRE: I think it's the costume that's throwing you. It threw me.

NICK: Yea right, the costume. That was for some other deal. But right here, right now, my role will be as it is normally, and that's detective. You can say investigation is my calling. Speaking of calling, do any of you folks have a cell phone with a clear signal?

LUDOS: What on earth for?

NICK: What for? (*sighs*) For calling? You know, here on earth? (*taps his mouth a few times*) Is this thing on? Testing? One, Two!

TRUCAGE: Coming through loud and clear!

NICK: Good. I need a phone that works loud and clear because... . Well, as I previously said we have a bit of thing here. A murdery type of deal.

TRUCAGE: I believe he means the Miss Heinspiele. You know, the poison fingers,

NICK: Wait! What? No, no! There were no poisoned fingers. It's more like strangled neck.

TRUCAGE: Strangled neck? (*To Ludos*) You said it was poison!

LUDOS: Did I? When did I say that?

TRUCAGE: A few moments ago. You said you were lead to believe it was poison on the lady fingers. Possibly meant for one of us. But she was strangled! (*Gasps*) Do you think the strangled neck was meant for one of us?

NICK: Yea, OK. Anyway, If we could get back to the matter at hand... do any of you have..

    DARLA enters quickly interrupting .

DARLA: Nick! Did you find a phone?

NICK: I was just working on that. We got a tad side tracked.

TRUCAGE: Sorry old chap. Don't think my cell phone works here.

LUDOS: What about the house phone? Why don't you use it, if it's so important?

DARLA: We did try it. The line is dead.

MENDACIO: I have one. I believe I left it upstairs. I'll just go fetch it shall I?

LUDOS: If you must, then please, by all means! I'm sure the detective would appreciate it.

TRUCAGE: Are you sure it works here? It probably doesn't.

MENDACIO: Well, I don't know.. I mean...

NICK: I sure would appreciate that.

Miss Mendacio crosses and exits up right

DARLA: And I'm sure your friend Miss Heinspiele would appreciate the care and concern you all are expressing for her. I mean, is it me?

NICK: Being snarky? Yea, I think it is.

DARLA: I think it's a little disconcerting that a women was strangled in the other room and you're all just sitting around playing Downton Abby!

DEIDRE: That's not what they're playing.

TRUCAGE: Well what are *you* playing at Detective person? What do you expect us to do? As you said, the phone doesn't work. The reception is negligent and the roads are in inferior condition due to the storm. Yes, it is a tragedy about Miss Heinspiele and well all feel dreadful probably, but what can be done, I ask you?

NICK: Well, for starters we can try to figure out what happened! And by "happened" I mean, whose hands *happened* to go around Miss Heinspiele's neck.

LUDOS: Well it's clear to me, Deidre was the last person to be with Miss Heinspiele.

DEIDRE: Yes, true. I was only with her for a moment. She asked for vanilla extract. I went to the pantry to retrieve said item. And when I returned she was... well, not needing the extract anymore.

NICK: How long were you away?

DEIDRE: Ten minutes at the most. I would have returned sooner but the light in the pantry was out, making it difficult to see. Fortunately, I knew where the candlesticks were, from having gotten them earlier.

NICK: While you were searching, did you see or hear anything within those ten minutes?

DEIDRE: Well since the pantry is another room off of the kitchen and since it was dark, I would not have seen anything. But... I do believe I heard Miss Heinspiele say something. I'm not certain... but I thought I heard her say... "Oh it's you."

TRUCAGE: Was it Quincannon? I thought it was when I said it.

LUDOS: Then why didn't you say, "Oh it's you Quincannon!" ?

DARLA: Because victims never say the killer's name. Haven't you seen that movie?

TRUCAGE: Which movie?

DARLA: All of them.

NICK: Who is this Quincannon anyway?

TRUCAGE: A gentleman from last year's event. Friendly chap. (*beat*) Or was.

LUDOS: He was a bit too friendly. And *was* not invited back this year after his behavior during the Red hour.

DARLA: And just what is this "red hour"?

TRUCAGE: Oh it's just a little mindless diversion to break up the evening. A chance to let our hair down and... I say!

Do you think Quincannon could be behind this? Because he was not invited this year?

NICK: And appoints himself a buzz kill for this year? Throws a sack over your head, fires a pistol, drags you off and then sneaks around back and strangles Miss Heinspiele? All because he wasn't invited?

TRUCAGE: Could be.

NICK: If it *could be* then that means there *would be* someone lurking around that shouldn't be here.

LUDOS: Nonsense! I should think he conducted his business and left. Why would he remain? I've heard of returning to the scene of the crime, but not remaining.

DARLA: Right! Who hangs around when they weren't invited? Right Nick? Who would do that?

NICK: : Right Darla I can't imagine! In the mean time, I want to take a look around. Deidre if you could show me the pantry.

DEIDRE: Sure. Right this way. (*begins to exit*)

NICK: Everyone else, if you could just hang and chill.

LUDOS: Hang and chill ?

DARLA: He means hang as in *hang out*.. as in.. stay here and chill as in... relax.

NICK: Right! What she said. Stay here. No one may leave this home! The game is at hand! Or.. a foot. The game is some body part!

NICK crosses and exits off with DEIDRE

END ACT ONE

52

Act 2

TRUCAGE, LUDOS are seated and DARLA paces

TRUCAGE: Well this is certainly playing out in an exciting way!

LUDOS: I don't know if I would call it exciting. I mean, do you honestly think someone would show up here and cause such a diversion?

DARLA: A diversion? A diversion from what?

TRUCAGE: Oh you know. These evenings have a usual pattern.

DARLA: They do?

TRUCAGE: Yes my dear girl, you know.

DARLA: Right. Right. Usual pattern.

TRUCAGE: And some of us enjoy a bit of well, skylarking if you will. Just a drop or two into the mix. That's how the red hour came to be. A little jollification borrowed from our sword foam days. I mean, how would it be if we gathered and just went about the same business, the same way? I for one wouldn't enjoy that!

MENDACIO enters with cell phone

MENDACIO: Oh excuse me! I don't show any little thing-a-ma jiggles on my phone so I guess it's not working.

She shows Darla – Darla takes it to examine

DARLA: Well, you don't have it turned on for one thing.

MENDACIO: I don't? Silly me! Another thing is that. I would have been down sooner but I couldn't find the short cut down through the kitchen.

DARLA: The short cut through the kitchen?

LUDOS: Yes. The back passage in the upper hall way that leads down to the kitchen. I believe it was the servants staircase. All those that have *been* here before know about it.

MENDACIO: I knew about it and couldn't find it. I just split the difference and came down the front.

TRUCAGE: I'm not sure I knew about it. Did I?

LUDOS: Anyway, most of our guests know about it. The details of the estate are included in our guidelines. Which are included in the announcement on our invitations.

DARLA: Invitations? (*is looking intent at Mendacio's cell phone*)

MENDACIO: Why the invitations to our event here at Chipping Cleghorn. You should know that Nurse Christie! May I have my phone back now?

DARLA: Oh! Of course! *(gives cell back)* Right! *(thinking -crosses downstage away from group)* Chipping Cleghorn? Where do I know that name?

DEIDRE *enters crossing to LUDOS, MENDACIO and TRUCAGE – They speak in a group as if out of ear shot of DARLA*

DEIDRE: *(to Ludos not accent)* Excuse me. I think there's a bit of a problem here.

DARLA speaks facing down stage not realizing they are not listening as she speaks- nor are they paying attention to her

DARLA: I think there's a bit of a problem or misunderstanding here.

LUDOS: *(speaking to Deidre)* What is the problem?

DARLA: OK, see the deal is.. about the invitations.

DEIDRE: First of all, they *(indicates Darla)* are *not* invited guests to our event.

DARLA: We aren't one of your guests.

DEIDRE: They actually *are* stranded travelers. Not PC's in our venture.

DARLA: Literally. We were on our way to a costume party and just came here hoping to use your phone.

DEIDRE: A real detective and a real nurse.

DARLA: We told Deidre when we arrived. I explained it but.. .

LUDOS: (*no accent*) Well that explains quite a bit.

DARLA: But maybe I wasn't clear.

DEIDRE: Yes, but it doesn't explain the fact that Trudy.. she actually *is* dead. Literally. Not as a part of the free from. But in actuality.

LUDOS: (*no accent*) You mean *real* real?

DEIDRE: Very real.

TRUCAGE: Trudy? Good Lord! But how did.. ? I thought that...

LUDOS: You're kidding!

DEIDRE: Wish I was. See for yourselves.

> *TRUCAGE, MENDACIO and LUDOS quickly exit off left – NICK enters at same time*

DARLA: I'm not sure what kind of gathering or party this is or whatever you people are doing here tonight. Let me be clear, whoever you think I may be, I'm not.

NICK: Well who are you then?

DARLA: (*turning to see they've left*) What? Where did they go?

NICK: They all went into the kitchen.

DARLA: But I was talking to them!

NICK: I know I heard you.

DARLA: Nick listen, there's something weird going on here.

NICK: I've heard you say that before also.

DARLA: I know, but here's the weird thing! I think i've figured it out. They keep calling me nurse Christie and the name of this place, Chipping Cleghorn! I know where I've heard that before. It's from a book! It's a fictional place in Agatha Christie stories.

NICK: How very fitting. I mean, what with the murder and all.

DARLA: Don't you understand? The bad accents, the bizarre conversations! It's as if we stepped into some fictional world. Look at how complacent they are acted when they learned their friend was strangled. Whatever weird thing they're doing here, they think we're a part of it! You the detective and me the nurse. We apparently fit in to it! They think we're a part of whatever this is.   But we aren't! We're just here for a phone

NICK: Right! Just a phone! Is that too much?

DARLA: Mendacio went up to get her phone, acting as if she didn't have it all night! But I'm sure she been using it.

NICK: Using it? How do you know?

DARLA: She had texts from tonight. I only saw one that said something like "Juno or Tru-no.. Ink.. itches... or something. It's all creep to the tenth power.

NICK: You may have something there Darla dear. Are you finished with your something because I have something too.

DARLA: What's your something?

NICK: OK. Check it out.   *(searches pockets)* When I was out there in the kitchen with Deidre checking out the pantry I heard her talking, I thought she was speaking to me so I popped out of the pantry and saw she was talking to Heinspiele. I saw her bend down to check for a pulse. And then she looked white as a ghost and said something like, '*This is real! Trudy is really dead*.'

DARLA: Really dead? As opposed to what? Dubiously dead?

NICK: Long story short, I assured her that the death was very real, I was indeed a very real detective and our being here tonight was really an accident-stance. I think it finally sunk in. She got it. Now hopefully they all get it. (*pulls out notebook*) Ah! Got it!

DARLA: I was trying explain it them also but they all left and... wait! Won't they contaminate they crime scene?

NICK: It should be all right. I secured the body best I could. (*consults notebook*)   I believe Heinspiele was strangled with something. There are ligature marks on her neck not much in the way of fingerprints.   She was lying face down. And strange note, there was a little red towel placed on her back. Not sure what the deal is there.

DARLA: We've got to find out what's going on here Nick!

NICK: Said the person who keeps wanting to leave!

DARLA: It's time we went to work and got the bottom of this nutty night.

NICK: Right. I need to check the grounds for footprints or any sign of someone else.

DARLA: There's a passage! They were telling me there's a servants staircase that leads to the kitchen.

NICK: OK You check that out, I'll check outside. If I'm not back in 20 minutes, then.. I probably needed more time, so add another 10 or 15.

DARLA: No problem.

They Exit - lights down

Lights up

LUDOS, TRUCAGE, MENDACIO and DEIDRE are standing around. Their demeanor is different –and they speak naturally – no accents

MENDACIO: Well, this is a problem! That means that we... What do we do now? Split the prize?

TRUCAGE: This is definitely a monkey wrench thrown into the works. Maybe Melinda is right. I guess we should call the evening done. In light of the circumstances. Who was the Game Master on this one?

DEIDRE: I am. Or was.

TRUCAGE: *(to Ludos)* I thought *you* were GM Emily.

LUDOS: No, I was Game Master last month. When we did "Curse Of the Last Will".

TRUCAGE: Well this whole thing was a bust! I mean, most of the people didn't show up because of the weather. It's hard playing this out with only a few of us.

LUDOS: Yes and there were a *few* weren't actually a part of it.

TRUCAGE: Fooled me. But I admit, they fit in quite nicely. Especially that nurse. Hot-see Tot-see!

LUDOS: Edwin! It is exactly that kind of thing that got Quincannon banned from our events. His inappropriate actions with the women during the red hour.

MENDACIO: So we think it was him? He came back and strangled Trudy?

DEIDRE: What would he have against Trudy?

TRUCAGE: Maybe he was being inappropriate. I mean he always seem to have a thing for her. Maybe he got a little too, you know, hands on and she spurned his advances and he... well..didn't take it very well.

LUDOS: And what was this business about him grabbing you at the door and shooting a gun?

TRUCAGE: Why would I make up something like that? I have the bruises to prove it.

LUDOS: Speaking of real, how do we know this detective is real? Did anyone see a badge?

DEIDRE: I have no reason to doubt him. But he may have good reason to doubt us. I mean, what must he think of us? Here we are, playing out our (/) game and..

TRUCAGE: They can't blame us! We thought they were part of it! No telling what they thought of us. Probably thought we were a bunch of loonies.

DEIDRE: We should probably explain. I believe one them is upstairs. (*exits*)

TRUCAGE: Very well. Shall we find them and...?

MENDACIO: I don't know about you but I could use some coffee first

TRUCAGE: Yes! As could I. I would even split the last Danish with someone.

MENDACIO: I'll split it with you.

TRUCAGE: Fine. We can.. talk about.. things.

     MENDACIO, TRUCAGE and LUDOS exits left. After a few beats DARLA enters right, She is holding some papers (legal size) reading them over. She is reading silently and then begins reading out loud

DARLA: Player characters? Heinspiele, Trudy Osbourne? Captain Trucage.. Edwin Murphy? Melinda Stahlhaus..? What on earth? (*continues reading*) Rules and boundaries shall be as follows... death will be determined by a red flag... clues will be set on hour before...

DARLA crosses quickly right as if to run out toward front door, just as she does NICK enters they almost collide.

NICK: Darla! Funny running into you here!

DARLA: NICK! Stop doing that! (*smacks him with papers*) Here! Look at this. I found it upstairs. (*hands him papers*)

NICK: What's this? More dirt on the crazed killer? (*begins reading*)

DARLA: In a manner of speaking. That explains a lot! The bad accents. The bizarre behavior. The crazy newspaper! Everything! Read it!

NICK: I'm trying! (*takes a few beats to read*) It's instructions of some sort. And.. rules of (/) some..

DARLA: None of this is real! It's all fake. The newspaper. The killer! It's a larp!

NICK: A lard?

DARLA: No Larp! A game! It's all been a game! The winner stands to receive 10,000 dollars!

NICK: What 'chu talkin bout Willis?

LUDOS enters from left

LUDOS: Oh. Here you are. I thought I heard someone.

Darla takes paper from Nick and consults it.

DARLA: Yes! Here we are. Nick, may I introduce Emily Brent!

NICK: Brent? I thought her name was Ludos.

DARLA: Emily has been assuming the role of Miss Ludos this evening. It's her PC or Player character in the game.

Trucage enters.

NICK: Her player character ?

TRUCAGE: Oh! Here they are!

DARLA: And this is Edwin Murphy who has been identifying as Captain Montgomery Trucage

NICK: Has he? OK. Hi. How's it goin?

TRUCAGE: (EDWIN): Pretty well. Yourself?

NICK: Not bad. Can't complain.

TRUCAGE: (To Ludos) So, the truth is out.

LUDOS (EMILY) : Yes, it's reared it's ugly head.

DEIDRE enters

DARLA: And this should be Vera Claythorne.

NICK: And Jerry Mathers as the beaver.

DEIDRE (VERA) : So, they know now I take it?

NICK: Yes! Yes, we know now! *(turns to Darla)* OK Help me out here Darla. What do we know?

DARLA: *(reading) A Mystery Night At Cleghorn.* An evening of murder and thievery! A role playing game for up to 10 guests or more.

NICK: A game? You mean you people have playing... this has all been...

LUDOS (EMILY) : You must forgive us. Apparently there has been a misunderstanding.

DARLA: A game Nick. It's has been a LARP.

NICK: Of course it is! Naturally. Any fool could see that its... (*Beat*) What is it?

DEIDRE (VERA) : A Larp stands for *Live Action Role Play*. Think of it like this.. imagine the old board game of Clue but on a larger scale. Played out in live action. Real people We all assume roles in the game and act it out.

NICK: Oh. Like D and D? *(begins digging in pockets for notepad)*

DEIDRE (VERA) : Right. But without the dragons, dungeons and swords. We each assume different characters within a game. And play out a particular scenario.

DARLA: That explains the bad accents and bizarre behavior!

DEIDRE (VERA) : We each assume a character that has a list of goals. Edwin was Captain Trucage. Petty thief with questionable intentions. Emily was Miss Ludos, the stock matron and I was Deidre the sarcastic domestic of the estate.

DARLA: So, whose estate is this?

DEIDRE (VERA) : It belongs to Emily. She is kind enough to allow us use of her home here.

LUDOS (EMILY) : It's very fitting for our games. Which of course we make up as we go. None of us really know what the others will say or do that's what makes it fun! We get together a few times a year and have this event. It livens up this dreary old place.

TRUCAGE: (EDWIN): You never can tell what will happen. Heck, half the time we don't know who will turn up and be a part of it.

DEIDRE (VERA) : Hence the confusion with you. This particular game included stranded travelers.

LUDOS (EMILY) : A nurse and a detective. But apparently the weather prevented everyone from being here.

DARLA: Except us. The real stranded travelers. The real detective and nurse.

NICK: What a Co-winkie-dink huh? And apparently we have a real murder. What are the odds?

DARLA: So was Heinspiele or Trudy supposed to be the victim tonight?

DEIDRE (VERA) : Actually that's the thing. Anyone can be the victim, it's not set in stone. This is a free form game meaning anything can happen. I was the Game master tonight, which means I am in charge and oversee all elements of the story we create. I verify game casualties.

DARLA: How do you verify? How do you know someone is dead in the game?

DEIDRE (VERA) : A red flag or tea towel is placed on the victim signifying a kill. Since anyone of us are qualified to be the killer, we all carry one. To.. you know, remove someone from the game.

MENDACIO enters from left

MENDACIO: There you are! I didn't know where everyone went! I thought we were going up the back stairs.. I turned around and everyone was gone.

LUDOS (EMILY) : I believe you all know Melinda Stahlhaus.

MENDACIO (MELINDA): *(still using an accent)* Delighted to make your acquaintance!

LUDOS (EMILY) : You can cut it Mel. They know. We told them.

MENDACIO (MELINDA): Told them? Told them what?

TRUCAGE (EDWIN): Nothing too scandalous. Just that we are just players in a game.

NICK: Yes. Players in a game. Of course! *(still searching pockets)* So let me paste this Jackson Pollack together into a clearer picture. This evening was all shuck and jive. Pretend. Play acting. A game of simulated mystery. Someone becomes a *make believe* victim and someone would be a *make believe* killer. (*finally finds notepad -now searches for pencil)*

DEIDRE (VERA) : Correct. And the goal of the game would be one or more of us figuring out who the killer is.

DARLA: Who *was* the killer in this game?

DEIDRE (VERA) : It could be anyone. Nothing is set in stone. It just plays out as we go. That's the fun of free form games. Anyone can be the victim and anyone might be the killer.

NICK: But *this* game played out with a deadly role of the die. Heinspiele wasn't a role play victim but a real time victim. So it goes without saying... but I will, there is a real time killer.

TRUCAGE: (EDWIN):   Some one in this very room!

MENDACIO (MELINDA): Or someone *outside* this room.

NICK: Speaking of which, I did check outside. *(consults notes)* Fortunately, our torrential downpour is now just a trivial dampening. I did find a set of footprints, which I believe were yours.. Captain...uh..

TRUCAGE: (EDWIN): Edwin. Or Eddy is fine.

NICK: OK Captain Eddie. I also found what I believe to be a second set of prints. Let me ask you, this person who grabbed you, was he a heavy set guy, medium or smallish?

TRUCAGE: (EDWIN): Well, I would say.. the person was by no means a little. They over powered me!

NICK: I also found some footprints around the back leading to the kitchen door. Which would appear to be a different size and than the Captains here. A tad larger.

LUDOS (EMILY) : *(gasps)* So this person came in the back into the kitchen and killed Trudy?

NICK: Maybe. Maybe not. They left track up to the door but no muddy tracks on the kitchen floor. Perhaps they took off their shoes. Or there is a chance someone came down the back stairs or was hiding in the kitchen.

MENDACIO (MELINDA): Maybe in the pantry!

NICK: Well no, because Deidre or whoever was in the food pantry at the time. I believe the only thing hiding in there is way too many expired cans of creamed corn. Although that pantry is large, you could park 3 Buicks and range rover in there.

LUDOS (EMILY) : I thought you said the light was out. How did you see anything?

NICK: I always carry a light emitting diode. (*shows a small flashlight*) Standard issue for a detective.   I found the light bulb had been broken. Funny that huh? While exploring outside I saw that the phone line had been tampered with. Bulbs broke, lines fiddled with, all very classic in cases like this. Was this part of your game?

TRUCAGE: (EDWIN): That would have been good! But no. Not part of our game. I don't think.

DARLA: But part of someone's game. Now if Trudy were the intended target, I have to wonder, how would they know that she would be going into the kitchen?

MENDACIO (MELINDA): That's true! Anyone might have gone out there. It could have been me.

LUDOS (EMILY) : Or me. I did go out to the kitchen to tell Trudy the red hour was starting.

MENDACIO (MELINDA): And I went out to flip the circuit breaker! I was there in the dark! It's a wonder I made it out alive!

LUDOS (EMILY) : But what about the footprints leading to the back door! That must mean they came in through the back door

DARLA: Or maybe they came down the back staircase.

MENDACIO (MELINDA): Or came in the back door and went up the back stairs. Or down the back stairs and out the door. Or maybe (/) they went...

LUDOS (EMILY) : Thank you Melinda. We get the picture.

NICK: Let's look at the *big* picture with a little paint by numbers, if you will. The fist color will be motive and I'm sure in your games you're familiar with that little nugget. So, who had it in for Heinspiele.

LUDOS (EMILY) : Her real name was Trudy. She was a sweetheart. Not an evil bone in her body. I can't think of anyone who *had it in* for her.

TRUCAGE: (EDWIN): I had nothing against her. I've done many of these events with her. A great player! How about you Vera?

DEIDRE (VERA) : No. I only knew her from the games here. Not socially outside of there.

TRUCAGE: (EDWIN): Melinda?

MENDACIO (MELINDA): Me? Absolutely not! Not in a millions years! I can't think of anyone here who would want to strangle Trudy.

NICK: OK our next color is opportunity. Let's paint some happy little bushes with that. When our victim went out into the kitchen, the rest of you were.... ?

LUDOS (EMILY) : Well I was right here. In this room that is. And so was Vera and Melinda.

MENDACIO (MELINDA):That's right! It was time for the red hour. We were all right here. But.. (*To Ludos*) Emily, you did go out there to tell here the red hour was starting.

LUDOS (EMILY) : Well yes, but I was only there for a moment. Not long enough to... do anything.

NICK: (to Mendacio) And you went out to flip the circuit breaker?

MENDACIO (MELINDA): Well, yes. I.. I did. But it was dark as you know. I followed the wall with my hand. I called out to Trudy. I said, "Hi Trudy, it's me Melinda. I'm trying to find the circuit breaker." And she said. "Let me." Or something.

DARLA: Did you hear her say, *Oh it's you* or someone stumbling?

MENDACIO (MELINDA): The stumbling was me. I almost fell in front of the sink. I think there was something on the floor.

TRUCAGE: (EDWIN): It may have been your own two feet. *(beat)* Lord knows I have done that in the dark.

NICK: When the lights came back on where was Trudy? Where was she standing?

MENDACIO (MELINDA): She was at the fuse box. I assume she did it herself. The lights that is. And she was very much alive at that time! I mean, otherwise I doubt she could have flipped the switch. She was just standing there.

NICK: Where do we stand?   We have a portrait of motive and opportunities, now we need to frame it. I would like each of you to explore this place. Look for anything out of place or any clues. Imagine your playing your game. But of course, you *were.* Look upstairs and all around.

MENDACIO (MELINDA): And what are we looking for?

LUDOS (EMILY) : Clues Melinda. And I suppose anyone hiding.

NICK: Yes. Brilliant. Look for anyone or anything that doesn't belong. Minus of course, Darla and me.

TRUCAGE: (EDWIN): Great idea! Ladies if you want me to take the lead. You know, just in case!

LUDOS (EMILY) : Very good Edwin. Lead away!

      TRUCAGE: (EDWIN) exits off right followed by LUDOS (EMILY), DEIDRE (VERA) and MENDACIO (MELINDA) - NICK and DARLA remain.

DARLA: So what are we going to do?

NICK: Wait and see what they do. If anyone of them is guilty, here is the part where they panic and make a mistake.

DARLA: But what about this mysterious Quincannon guy? Are you really entertaining that?

NICK: It's a possibility I suppose! There were some extra footprints outside.

DARLA: And you think he would sneak in through the back door and strangled Trudy?

NICK: Could be. And he could be part of the game

DARLA: What do you mean, part of the game?

NICK: Well if it's like they said, free form, and they just make it up as they go, maybe someone is making up quite a few extra bits and bobs tonight.

DARLA: How do we know what is real and what's the game?   How do we tell?

NICK: Become a player!

DARLA: That's stupid Nick!

NICK: I think the saying is, don't hate the player, hate the game! So let's you and I go outside and play bit of hide and seek.

DARLA: But it's muddy. I don't want to get my shoes dirty. They cost a (/) lot of..

NICK: I think you may be onto something dear Darla! The game really is *a foot.* Follow me! This I what I want you to do....

   NICK speaks silently to DARLA as they exit off left

Lights down

Lights up

TRUCAGE: (EDWIN) enters from right followed by MENDACIO (MELINDA) and DEIDRE (VERA)

MENDACIO (MELINDA): Well, I didn't find anything or anyone.

TRUCAGE: (EDWIN): Nope. Me either. Everything was right where it was.

DEIDRE (VERA) : Do we know what happened to the necklace?

MENDACIO (MELINDA): Necklace? What necklace?

DEIDRE (VERA) : From the game. That one was taken.

TRUCAGE: (EDWIN): Oh that! Right. I know where that is. (*looks around*) Where did I...? Oh! I remember.

EDWIN goes to couch and lifts cushion. He feels around. Lifts another searching.

TRUCAGE: (EDWIN): (*cont.*) It was right here! I swear I stuck it in here.

MENDACIO (MELINDA): Maybe someone.. took it!

TRUCAGE: (EDWIN): Yes. *Me!* I took it. I'm the petty thief character.

DEIDRE (VERA) : I think she means... someone *else*. As in stole it *from* you.

TRUCAGE: (EDWIN): Who would steal something I already stole?! That makes no sense!

DEIDRE (VERA) : It makes no sense killing Trudy either.

TRUCAGE: (EDWIN): No. No it doesn't. Why I should worry about a silly necklace? (*beat*) I guess now, with Trudy being... you know, that we.... I mean, I guess that eliminates the overall prize. What are the rules about this Vera? I can't remember.

DEIDRE (VERA): When there's no winner, there's a split between players

TRUCAGE: (EDWIN): There certainly is no winner here. So, it would be five ways then? Or four I guess.

DEIDRE (VERA) : I was the Game Master so technically, I'm out. It would be three ways.

MENDACIO (MELINDA): But you should get something Vera. It almost doesn't seem right to do.

LUDOS (EMILY) enters from right.

LUDOS (EMILY) : What doesn't seem right?

TRUCAGE (EDWIN): Everything about this night. Did you find anything?

LUDOS (EMILY) : No I didn't. The only thing I found is this to be the worst event ever!

DEIDRE (VERA):   I know Emily. I feel awful about what happened. Maybe the detective has found something.

TRUCAGE: (EDWIN): I doubt it.

>   *NICK enters from left .*

NICK: Hello peeps, how's it going? Anything to report? *(takes out small notebook)*

TRUCAGE: (EDWIN): Nothing on my end. I searched this place top to bottom.

>   *NICK makes notes through out following*
exchanges

NICK: That would include all of your personal belongings? Your clothes or do you come dressed in costume all ready?

DEIDRE (VERA) : Yes. We come dressed for the occasion.

NICK: Shoes as well?

DEIDRE (VERA) : Yes. The idea of the game to enter in character and leave in character.

NICK: And as these characters, you make it up as you go and whatever happens, *happens* right?

DEIDRE (VERA) : Well yes, for the most part. But we have guidelines, a theme..

LUDOS (EMILY) : For instance, this particular game had an Agatha Christie theme. A Murder Has Been Announced or Ten Little Indians, something along those lines.

NICK: And within those lines, how do you win this game?

DEIDRE (VERA): Well,   the players guess the murderer. If they think they know, they write it down and place it in the "Guess" jar. Whoever is the first to guess correctly, wins.

NICK: A guess jar? We have a swear jar at my house. Anyway, who monitors this Guess Jar?

DEIDRE (VERA): That would be me. I check the jar frequently and make notes.

NICK: And when you guess correctly and become the winner, you get the big prize money.

LUDOS (EMILY) : Yes. Ten thousand dollars.

NICK: And where does this money come from?
DEIDRE (VERA) : Entry fees. Each player pays around thousand to play.

LUDOS (EMILY) : We were expecting ten guests this evening but...

NICK: But what if no one wins. No one guesses correctly?

DEIDRE (VERA): The victim gets the money.

NICK: Hmmm. Interesting. I'm sure it's probably in your rules. Darla was showing me the... Speaking of which, where did my wife get to? Darla? Oh Darla?

Darla enters from right.

DARLA: Yes! I'm here. I was finishing up... doing the.. you know... thing.

NICK: Brilliant! OK. I'm developing a pretty good idea here in my handy dandy notebook. And as a wise man once said, "Eliminate the impossible, and whatever remains, however improbable must be the truth" . The truth here, is that you all have remained. I would like to continue *the game*. And what I mean, is I would like you all to cast your vote. To use your guess jar.

LUDOS (EMILY) : Use the guess jar to vote?

DARLA: Yes. Play along. Just as you would have in your *Mystery Night At Cleghorn.*

MENDACIO (MELINDA): But so many strange things have happened outside of the normal game. And besides, I thought that this Quincannon man was (/) the...

TRUCAGE: (EDWIN): Yes! Melinda has a valid point! The game is off the rails. I say until this Quincannon business is sorted out, that we (/)can't really..

NICK: Due to reasons I won't go into now, I want you to take old Quinty out of the running. Out of the picture. Forget him. Only vote for the people in this room. (*beat*) That is, except for Darla and Me. You know, because, well. It would be silly, really.

LUDOS (EMILY) : But in our game we have clues! And a clear idea of some sort!

DARLA: Just consider the facts. Several people went out into the kitchen when Trudy was there. Oh sure, they said they spoke with her and everything was fine but..how do you know? How much do you really trust each other? That's what we would like to find out by your votes.

TRUCAGE: (EDWIN): You want us to do this.. now?

MENDACIO (MELINDA): Where's the guess jar?

DEIDRE (VERA) : I believe it 's upstairs.

LUDOS (EMILY) : Very well! Let's get to it.

They all exit off Right – ad libbing with each other. At this point the audience can be invited to Vote. NICK and DARLA can break the 4th wall and handle instructions or if you wish to keep the 4 walls closed – someone else can. The cast can help collect votes.

LUDOS (EMILY) , TRUCAGE: (EDWIN), DEIDRE
(VERA) and MENDACIO (MELINDA) all gather on stage
– sitting etc..

NICK and DARLA enter – Darla carries jar with (cast)
votes. Nick searches for and finds his notepad.

NICK: Welcome back my friends to the show that never
ends! My lovely assistant Darla has your votes and as to
who the winner is... well, it's anybody's guess.

MENDACIO (MELINDA): What about your guess? You're
the detective.

NICK: Yes. Yes I am. I spent 15 years on the force before
going into private work.

TRUCAGE: (EDWIN): So you're a private eye?

NICK: That I am.

LUDOS (EMILY) : So, you were in homicide before, I take
it?

NICK: No. Narcotics. But it doesn't matter. I can still
detect facts. But enough about me. Let's get back your
facts shall we? Who is our first contestant tonight Darla?

DARLA: *(taking paper slip from jar)* Our first contestant
is.... *(reads)* Emily Brent!

NICK: Emily Brent! Come on down!

LUDOS (EMILY) : What? I don't understand why I even have a vote! I wasn't in the kitchen with Trudy. The logistics don't play out.

NICK: You are correct Emily!. Although you stated you went out to let Trudy know that the Red hour was about to begin, I think it's not very likely you're the evil doer. Our next contestant!

DARLA: *(taking paper slip from jar)* Our next contestant is... *(reads)* Vera Claythorne.

LUDOS (EMILY) : Right! Vera was the GM, so technically not eligible.

MENDACIO (MELINDA): She was in the kitchen with Trudy!

NICK: Yes she was. However, Vera was the one who discovered Trudy's true fate. Ask yourself why would a killer announce to everyone their victim's demise?

MENDACIO (MELINDA): Well, to throw suspicion away from themselves.

NICK: That only happens in the movies, right Darla?

DARLA: In about twenty that I can think of. Cut back to you Nick.

NICK: Fade in on our next vote.

DARLA: *(taking paper slip from jar)* And we zoom in on... (reads) Vera Claythorne again!

NICK: What do you guys have against poor Vera?

TRUCAGE: (EDWIN): As Melinda said, she was really the only one with opportunity. I was accosted at (/) the door and....

LUDOS (EMILY) : Please Ed! We've heard the story too many times now.

NICK: She's right! Too many stories we have all heard before. My own wife tried to point that out to me earlier tonight. This night is riddled with cliches. Let me present one more cliché, follow the money and you'll find your culprit.

TRUCAGE: (EDWIN): Money? What money? There's no money. No one actually won! The game is over.

DARLA: Is it? As I understand the rules, you all will now split the prize four ways.

TRUCAGE: (EDWIN): Three ways.

NICK: Which ain't bad for a nights work. But I think some of you had your heart set on splitting it 2 ways. Which ain't bad to boot. Or should I say shoe! *(beat)* That's your first cue Darla.

DARLA: Right! Sorry. (*she hurries off left exits)*

LUDOS (EMILY) : What is this about?

NICK: This is about game theory, or my theories about your game night. (*consults notepad*) Now as I understand this, when the murder happens in your game, you place a red flag on the victim. And you each carry a red cloth, because *anyone* could be the killer. One was used on Trudy to signify her death. So, may I see your cloths?

> *Everyone except DEIDRE (VERA) pulls out their* red cloth.

DEIDRE (VERA) : Of course, I do not carry one because I was the game master.

TRUCAGE: (EDWIN): And we all have ours!

NICK: Trudy was a player correct? Therefore she would've had a red cloth of her own. We could assume, her own cloth was placed on her.

TRUCAGE: (EDWIN): Oh. Right. Of course. That makes sense.

NICK: But! What doesn't make sense is, the red cloth on Trudy was rather damp. Of course, I realize she was in the kitchen and kitchens are places where water and dampness can be a thing, but we can't ignore the fact that water and dampness have been running amuck outside tonight. So we have a missing necklace and damp cloth. What does that add up to?

MENDACIO (MELINDA): Ummmm.... Maybe someone dropped their red cloth...in the sink?

LUDOS (EMILY): Or maybe it came from outside.

TRUCAGE: (EDWIN): Maybe we should wait till the authorities get here and sort it all out.

NICK: And maybe someone here will have more time to cover their tracks. Trust me. It all adds up. Melinda, may I borrow your phone for a minute, I want to use your calculator?

MENDACIO (MELINDA): (*reluctantly*) Ummm.. sure I guess. (*hands it to him*)

NICK: Thank you. Let's see, (*going through phone*) The square root of murder, times pie... carry the one. Ah ha!

TRUCAGE: (EDWIN): What are you doing?

DARLA enters holding a pair of men's shoes.

DARLA: Got 'em!

LUDOS (EMILY) : Whose are those?

DARLA: We believe they belong to our elusive visitor Mr Quincannon!

MENDACIO (MELINDA): So he *was* here!

DARLA: Only in spirit. You see, Nick and I believe this Mr Quincannon was actually played by someone else here.

NICK: Why you ask? Go ahead ask.

MENDACIO (MELINDA): OK. Why?

NICK: Good question! If you can make it up as you and anything can happen, why not make something happen will benefit the needs of the few.

LUDOS (EMILY) : What do you mean, needs of the few?

NICK: What if someone made their own little game inside the big game? A little game of I'll let you murder me and then I create a diversion so crazy it ll throw everyone off. No one will guess the killer. And if no one guesses correctly, per the rules, the victim gets the grand prize. And then the victim splits it with the killer.

LUDOS (EMILY): OK but how would you throw everyone off?

NICK: Easy. Just like it was accomplished tonight. Introduce the potential for a mystery guest. One who comes and knocks on the door. Fires some blanks so that gun shots are heard. Leaves footprints for us to find. Foot prints that don't match anyone here. No body is found. The game is a draw. And the prize is split between the conspirators.

DARLA: And this is usually the part where the guilty party panics and stands up (/) and

TRUCAGE: (EDWIN): (*stands*) All right! Hold the phone! Are you suggesting that I made up the whole thing to throw everyone off by pretending to be shot and then hid in the shed so they couldn't find me!

NICK: Yes Captain Eddie, we were pretty much suggesting that! Spot on old boy! We are also suggesting that you had an accomplice. Who placed men's shoes on. Snuck out the back, came around to the front, (/) where...

DARLA: Where she knocked at the front door. If you recall,I was here at the time and you went to answer. Shots were fired so that I would hear them and see you, concluding you had been the victim in the game. And you disappeared so the rules of the game could be tested!

TRUCAGE: (EDWIN): What? That's nonsense!

NICK: I found the pistol loaded with blanks out behind the shed.

DARLA: And I found these shoes and this under the sink. Shoes your accomplice used.

NICK: But here's the crazy bit. The funny part of the story. I think you did something foolish. Something wacky. Dare I say careless. I think you became bored waiting out there and tried to sneak around to the kitchen.

Perhaps feeling parched or peckish. Or maybe need to relay a message. Whatever the case, while you were there Trudy came out and almost saw you.

DARLA: You ducked into the pantry. Breaking the light bulb so you couldn't be seen. While there you sent a desperate text message to your accomplice.

NICK: In your panic you left the shoes by the sink. Along with your red cloth.

DARLA: And this! (*holds up necklace*)

TRUCAGE: (EDWIN): But I put that under the cushions in the couch!

NICK: I'm sure you did. At some point earlier. But you or your accomplice retrieved it again. And you probably made sure others were around went you went to "pretend" to retrieve it, making it seem that someone had taken it. Again throwing everyone off your trail.

TRUCAGE: (EDWIN): What are you implying detective? If you're trying to say that I or someone strangled Trudy with that necklace?

DEIDRE (VERA) : He didn't imply that.

LUDOS (EMILY) : No Edwin. He didn't. *You* did.

TRUCAGE: (EDWIN): I did? Well, darn it!   But.. but... where's your proof?!

NICK: Right here on Melinda's phone. These text messages.

MENDACIO (MELINDA): *(tries to grab phone)* Oh that! That's nothing.

NICK: *(reading from Melinda phone)* Tru-nose.. In kitch... .. left red flag shoe in kitch plea get! Will creet diversion front. Around neck and Kill her. Which I believe translates very roughly into . *Trudy knows. She's in the kitchen, left red flag and shoes. Please get. I will create a diversion around the front. Get Necklace. And Kill her.*

TRUCAGE: (EDWIN): It was supposed to say "Tell Her"! Not *kill* her! Bloody auto correct!

MENDACIO (MELINDA): I didn't know!

TRUCAGE: (EDWIN): Why would I say *kill her*? Stupid woman! We could have had a 3 way split with Trudy. You just had to tell her! She would've been in on it! All because you strangled her!

MENDACIO (MELINDA): You said *around neck*!

TRUCAGE: (EDWIN): I meant the necklace! I'll go around front! Get the necklace! It was dark I could see the letters!

DEIDRE (VERA) : Wait! You were going to trick us and split the prize!

LUDOS (EMILY) : Do you mean to tell me that you two killed Trudy!

TRUCAGE: (EDWIN): I didn't! *She* did!

MENDACIO (MELINDA): It's not my fault you can't spell! Also not my fault you left the stupid red flag on the sink! And the shoes! I fell over them!

TRUCAGE: (EDWIN): And it's not my fault you can't delete your messages!

MENDACIO (MELINDA): I didn't have time! I was lucky I could get out in the kitchen to clean your mess!

DARLA: Because Trudy saw what you left in the sink. Perhaps she even saw you lurking in the kitchen. It wouldn't take long for her to figure it out. To figure out the scenario you had come up with. She would tell Vera and you little cheating plan would have failed

DEIDRE (VERA) : And you would have been disqualified.

TRUCAGE: (EDWIN): Not if Melinda would told her!

LUDOS: (EMILY): I doubt she would have fallen for your trickery. She never would have been a part of it!

TRUCAGE (EDWIN): We'll never know now, will we Melinda?

DEIDRE (VERA) : (to Edwin) But why did you come back in? With that Quincannon story about being tied up? What was that all about?

NICK: A little more free form improvising on his part. You see his first plan hid a major snag. He needed a way to cover his tracks. Probably found some rope and a gag and came up with goofy kidnap story. In the mean time, you wanted poor Mel to convince Trudy to play along. A three way split. But alas. Epic fail.

DARLA: What else could he do but try to salvage the game by reappearing and trying to cover up his cheats. He made up his crazy Quincannon story to cover the footprints he had Melinda plant. He had to explain them now. He knew we would find them. Introduce a new story for the evening. With Trudy on board, perhaps the creepy Quincannon could reappear and claim a new victim. He could place his red flag on her in the kitchen. You all would have been so confused no one could guess the killer.

TRUCAGE: (EDWIN): It would have worked too!

DARLA: Right if hadn't been for those meddling kids!

NICK: That and a deadly typo.

TRUCAGE: (EDWIN): I swear I put "Tell her!" not "Kill her!" So technically, I'm innocent.

NICK: I'm sure a judge and jury will have fun with that one. (*dials out on Mel's phone*)

LUDOS (EMILY) : In all my years of these events, this has to be craziest outcome ever! To think you thought you could get away with something like this !

DARLA: They almost did. If they would have found a better disposal method for the shoes, the gun and the necklace. We might have never tied it all together.

TRUCAGE: (EDWIN): (*To Melinda*) Why did you throw them under the sink?!
MENDACIO (MELINDA): Why did you throw the gun behind the shed?

TRUCAGE: (EDWIN): You had plenty of time to (/) get rid..

MENDACIO (MELINDA): No I didn't! Vera was out there in the pantry!

TRUCAGE: (EDWIN): You could have left the lights out longer!

MENDACIO (MELINDA): She turned them on! And you could have talked to her yourself, instead running away like an idiot!

TRUCAGE: (EDWIN): Oh! I'm the idiot? I'm the idiot?

NICK: *(into phone)* Yes hello? This is private detective Nick Dashell. Hey, how's it going? *(Continues talking silently)*

MENDACIO (MELINDA): Why did you have to sneak in the kitchen? Why didn't you stay put?

DARLA: OK! Guys! Why don't we play a new game? It's called the quiet game or the right to remain silent. Melinda and Edwin you start!

DEIDRE (VERA) : I don't know what we would have done, if you two hadn't... shown up.

DARLA: Who knows. I'm sure even if our car didn't break down and we didn't wander in here, one of you would have spoiled their game.

DEIDRE (VERA) : I would like to believe so. For one thing I wasn't really buying that whole Quincannon story anyway. Some odd ball from last year showing up here.

    There is a knock at the door.

DARLA: Nick?! Nick! There's someone at the door!

NICK: *(covers phone)* What?

DARLA: The door! Someone knocking!

NICK: Well I'm not getting it this time! You get it Darla.

DARLA: Nick!

TRUCAGE: (EDWIN): That's OK! I'll get it!

He runs off quickly and MENDACIO (MELINDA): follows as if to escape.

DARLA: They're getting away! Nick! Nick!

NICK: Chill Darla. It's just the local PD. Someone in the area heard the gun shots earlier and called. That will be them checking on us. Every thing's cool. I'm arranging a tow truck now. Then we can get a ride and still have enough time to make the costume party!

DARLA: Wonderful. And this is the part where the female protagonist sighs with her arms crossed. And the camera zooms in on her face as she rolls her eyes.

Lights out

The End

Other Murder Mystery plays by Lee Mueller

A Plot Of Murder

An Audition For A Murder

Dead 2 Rights

Dead Air

Death Near Dead Man's Holler

Death Of A Doornail

I'm Getting Murdered In The Morning

Irritation To A Murder

Last Call At Chez Mort

Murder Me Always

Remains To Be Seen

Talk About A Murder

To Wake The Dead

53421910R00057

Made in the USA
Charleston, SC
08 March 2016